quick
cooking

TRIDENT
PRESS
INTERNATIONAL

Published by:
TRIDENT PRESS INTERNATIONAL
801 12th Avenue South
Suite 302
Naples, FL 34102 U.S.A.
Copyright (c)Trident Press International
Tel: (941) 649 7077
Fax: (941) 649 5832
Email: tridentpress@worldnet.att.net
Website: www.trident-international.com

acknowledgements

Quick Cooking

Compiled by: R&R Publications Marketing P/L
Creative Director: Paul Sims
Production Manager: Anthony Carroll
Food Photography: Warren Webb,
Andrew Elton, Quentin Bacon, Per Ericson,
Paul Grater, Ray Joice, John Stewart,
Ashley Mackevicius, Harm Mol,
Yanto Noerianto, Andy Payne.
Food Stylists: Wendy Berecry,
Michelle Gorry, Donna Hay.
Recipe Development: Ellen Argyriou,
Sheryle Eastwood, Lucy Kelly, Donna Hay,
Anneka Mitchell, Penelope Peel,
Jody Vassallo,Loukie Werle.
Proof Reader: Andrea Tarttelin

Includes Index
ISBN 1582790981
EAN 9781582790985

First Edition Printed June 2001
Computer Typeset in Humanist 521
& Times New Roman

Printed in Hong Kong

Contents

introduction

introduction

Quick cooking

More often than not fast food is associated with large food chains which turn out hamburgers, pizzas and fried chicken almost before you have had time to order!

Here you will find a wonderful selection of recipes that prove you can create great food at home and it need not take you hours. This book is for all those who yearn to eat real food, but do not have time to cook. A quick look at the recipes and ingredients will show you that it can be just as quick to cook at home as it is to stop at a takeaway food shop, with the added advantage that you know exactly what you are eating.

Every kitchen-tested recipe is superbly photographed and captures the flavour and diversity of modern cooking, using readily available ingredients and short cuts. You will find recipes for all occasions appetising ideas for fast dinners when running late, easy exotic stir-fries, tempting entrees and treats for the barbecue.

Photograph page 5 and recipe page 24 (Thigh Steaks with Fruity Salsa)

*camembert surprise in
banana sauce*

succulent

starters

Starters are far too good to be reserved

*for special occasions, however being light and easily
digestible, they make perfect lunch or supper dishes.
Simply adjust the quantities or reduce the number of
servings if more substantial portions are required.*

satay
style oysters

Method:

1 Place peanut butter, sour cream and Tabasco sauce to taste in a bowl and mix to combine.
2 Place oysters in a baking tin, place a spoonful of mixture onto each oyster and sprinkle with bacon. Cook under a preheated hot grill for 2-3 minutes or until oysters are golden. Sprinkle with parsley or coriander and serve.
Note: Serve as an entrée with a squeeze of fresh lemon or lime juice and buttered fresh brown bread.

ingredients

2 tablespoons smooth peanut butter
$^1/_3$ cup/90g/3oz sour cream
Tabasco sauce
12 fresh oysters, on the half shell
2 rashers bacon, chopped
chopped fresh parsley or coriander

camembert
surprise in banana sauce

Photograph page 7

Method:

1 Halve Camemberts horizontally. Sprinkle banana slices with lemon juice and arrange on four of the Camembert halves. Sprinkle with coconut and top with remaining cheese halves. Press together firmly.
2 Combine egg and milk. Dip each Camembert in flour, egg mixture and breadcrumbs. Repeat crumbing process. Chill until firm.
3 Cook in hot oil until golden. Drain on absorbent paper and serve with sauce.
4 To prepare sauce, peel and roughly chop bananas. Place into the bowl of a food processor, add coconut cream, cream, spice and lemon juice. Process until smooth. Serve sauce separately or spooned over Camembert.
Cook's tip: Use a toothpick to hold each Camembert together while preparing and cooking. Remove toothpick before serving.
Serves 4

ingredients

4 x 125g Camembert cheese
2 ripe bananas, peeled and sliced
lemon juice
2 teaspoons desiccated coconut
plain flour
1 egg, beaten
3 tablespoons milk
3 cups/375g dry breadcrumbs
polyunsaturated oil for cooking

Banana sauce
2 ripe bananas
$^1/_2$ cup/125 ml coconut cream
2 tablespoons cream
$^1/_4$ teaspoon ground mixed spice
1 teaspoon lemon juice

chicken
and corn chowder

Method:

1 *Heat oil in a saucepan over a medium heat, add onion and cook, stirring, for 4-5 minutes or until onion is soft. Add chicken and cook for 2 minutes longer or until chicken just changes colour.*

2 *Add potatoes and stock and bring to the boil. Reduce heat and simmer for 10 minutes or until potatoes are almost cooked. Stir sweet corn, milk, bay leaf and black pepper to taste into stock mixture and bring to the boil. Reduce heat and simmer for 3-4 minutes or until potatoes are cooked. Remove bay leaf. Stir in lemon juice, parsley, chives and black pepper to taste. Just prior to serving, sprinkle with Parmesan cheese.*

Note: *To chop the sweet corn, place in a food processor or blender and process using the pulse button until the sweet corn is coarsely chopped. Creamed sweet corn can be used in place of the kernels if you wish. If using creamed sweet corn there is no need to chop it.*

Serves 6

ingredients

**1 tablespoon vegetable oil
1 small onion, diced
250g/8oz boneless chicken breast
fillets, shredded
3 potatoes, chopped
3¹/₂ cups/875mL/1¹/₂pt chicken stock
315g/10oz canned sweet corn kernels,
drained and coarsely chopped
1¹/₄ cups/315mL/10fl oz milk
1 bay leaf
freshly ground black pepper
1 tablespoon lemon juice
2 tablespoons chopped fresh parsley
1 tablespoon snipped fresh chives
60g/2oz grated Parmesan cheese**

vegetable
bean soup

Method:

1 Heat oil in a large saucepan over a medium heat, add onions and cook, stirring, for 5 minutes or until onions are lightly browned.
2 Add carrots, potatoes and stock and bring to the boil. Reduce heat, cover and simmer for 30 minutes or until vegetables are tender.
3 Stir in beans, milk, dill, parsley and black pepper to taste and cook, stirring frequently, for 3-4 minutes or until heated through.

Serves 4

ingredients

2 tablespoons vegetable oil
3 onions, diced
3 carrots, diced
3 potatoes, diced
3 cups/750mL/1¼pt vegetable stock
315g/10oz canned cannellini beans,
drained and rinsed
½ cup/125mL/4 fl oz milk
2 tablespoons chopped fresh dill
1 tablespoon chopped fresh parsley
freshly ground black pepper

Oven temperature 200°C/400°F/Gas 6

french
onion flans

Method:

1 Line six individual flan tins with pastry. Melt butter in a frypan and cook onions until golden. Divide into six portions and spread over base of flans.

2 Combine eggs, sour cream, nutmeg and horseradish. Pour into flans. Top with cheese and bake at 200°C/400°F/Gas 6 for 20 minutes or until firm.

Cook's tip: If fresh dill is unavailable, substitute 1 teaspoon dried dill leaves or ¼ teaspoon ground dill.

Serves 6

ingredients

3 sheets prepared puff pastry, thawed
6 onions, sliced
60g/2oz butter
3 eggs, beaten
1³/₄ cups/435g sour cream
1 teaspoon ground nutmeg
1½ teaspoons horseradish relish
1½ cups/175g grated tasty cheese

succulent
starters

scampi
with basil butter

Method:

1 Cut scampi or yabbies in half, lengthwise.
2 To make Basil Butter, place butter, basil, garlic and honey in a small bowl and whisk to combine.
3 Brush cut side of each scampi or yabbie half with Basil Butter and cook under a preheated hot grill for 2 minutes or until they change colour and are tender. Drizzle with any remaining Basil Butter and serve immediately.

Serves 8

ingredients

**8 uncooked scampi or yabbies,
heads removed**

Basil butter
90g/3oz butter, melted
2 tablespoons chopped fresh basil
I clove garlic, crushed
2 teaspoons honey

brushetta

Method:

1 *Brush bread slices with oil, place under a preheated hot grill and toast both sides until golden. Rub one side of toasts with cut side of garlic cloves.*

2 *For Tomato and Basil Topping, top half the toast slices with some tomato, onion and basil, and grill for 1-2 minutes or until topping is warm.*

3 *For Eggplant and Feta Topping, brush eggplant (aubergine) slices with oil and cook under preheated hot grill for 3-4 minutes each side or until lightly browned. Top remaining toasts with eggplant (aubergine) slices and sprinkle with feta cheese and black pepper to taste. Cook under a preheated hot grill for 1-2 minutes or until topping is warm.*

Makes 16-20

ingredients

1 French bread stick, cut into 1 cm/¹/₂ in slices
2 tablespoons olive oil
2 cloves garlic, halved

Tomato and basil topping
2 tomatoes, sliced
1 red onion, sliced
2 tablespoons shredded basil leaves

Eggplant and feta topping
2 baby eggplant (aubergines), sliced
1 tablespoon olive oil
125g/4oz feta cheese, crumbled
freshly ground black pepper

asparagus and salmon salad

simple
salads

Fine food comes in many guises,

---

but seldom is it simpler to prepare, more flavoursome

or more packed with goodness than when it is gathered

from the garden or garnered from the greengrocer.

Oven temperature 180°C, 350°F, Gas 4

green
seed salad

Method:

1 Rub bread with cut side of garlic, brush both sides lightly with olive oil and cut into 2cm/¾in cubes. Place bread cubes on a non-stick baking tray and bake for 10 minutes or until bread is golden and crisp. Cool slightly.

2 Place sunflower, pumpkin and sesame seeds on a non-stick baking tray and bake for 3-5 minutes or until golden. Cool slightly.

3 Place salad leaves, avocados, tomatoes, tofu and oranges in a salad bowl and toss. Sprinkle with croûtons and toasted seeds.

4 To make dressing, place oil, lemon juice, chilli sauce, soy sauce and sesame oil in a bowl and whisk to combine. Drizzle dressing over salad and serve immediately.

Note: Sunflower, pumpkin and sesame seeds are available from health food shops or the health food section of larger supermarkets.

Serves 6

ingredients

3 slices wholemeal bread, crusts trimmed
1 clove garlic, halved
¹/₄ cup/60mL/2fl oz olive oil
3 tablespoons sunflower seeds
2 tablespoons pumpkin seeds
2 tablespoons sesame seeds
500g/1 lb assorted salad leaves
2 avocados, stoned, peeled and sliced
250g/8oz cherry tomatoes, halved
250g/8oz firm tofu, chopped
2 oranges, segmented

Chilli sesame dressing
¹/₄ cup/60 mL/2 fl oz vegetable oil
2 tablespoons lemon juice
1 tablespoon sweet chilli sauce
1 teaspoon soy sauce
1 teaspoon sesame oil

pesto
pasta salad

Method:

1 Cook pasta in boiling water in a large saucepan following packet directions. Drain, rinse under cold running water and set aside to cool completely.

2 Place pasta, tomatoes, snow pea (mangetout) sprouts or watercress and green pepper (capsicum) in a salad bowl and toss to combine.

3 To make dressing, place basil leaves, 3 tablespoons pine nuts, Parmesan cheese, garlic, mayonnaise and water in a food processor or blender and process until smooth. Spoon dressing over salad and sprinkle with remaining pine nuts.

Note: This salad looks pretty when made with attractive pasta shapes such as bows, spirals or shells. Choose the pasta to suit the other dishes you are serving, for example, if serving the salad with fish, shells would be the perfect choice.

Serves 6

ingredients

375g/12oz pasta of your choice
250g/8oz cherry tomatoes
125g/4oz snow pea (mangetout) sprouts
or watercress
1 green pepper (capsicum), chopped
2 tablespoons pine nuts

Pesto dressing
1 bunch fresh basil
3 tablespoons pine nuts
3 tablespoons grated Parmesan cheese
1 clove garlic, crushed
¹/₂ cup/125mL/4fl oz mayonnaise
2 tablespoons water

waldorf
salad

Method:

1 *Place green apples, red apple, celery, walnuts and parsley in a bowl and toss to combine.*

2 *Place sour cream, mayonnaise and black pepper to taste in a small bowl and mix to combine. Add mayonnaise mixture to apple mixture and toss to combine. Cover and chill.*
   Note: *This salad can be made in advance, but if making more than 2 hours ahead toss apples in 1 tablespoon lemon juice to prevent them from browning.*
   Serves 6

ingredients

2 large green eating apples, cored and diced
1 large red eating apple, cored and diced
3 stalks celery, diced
60g/2oz walnut pieces
1 tablespoon chopped fresh parsley
¹/₄ cup/60g/2oz sour cream
¹/₄ cup/60mL/2fl oz mayonnaise
freshly ground black pepper

thigh steaks with fruity
mint salsa

everyday
meals

Just because you're busy doesn't mean

you can't prepare stylish and tasty meals.
With these recipes you can have a delicious
dinner on the table in no time at all.

lemon
mustard drumsticks

ingredients

2 tablespoons lemon juice
2 tablespoons Italian dressing
I teaspoon freshly ground black pepper
I teaspoon Worcestershire sauce
¹/₂ teaspoon prepared mustard
500g/I lb chicken drumsticks
pinch ground paprika

Method:

1 Place lemon juice, dressing, black pepper, Worcestershire sauce and mustard in a small bowl and mix to combine. Brush mixture over chicken and sprinkle with paprika.

2 Place chicken under a preheated medium grill and cook, turning frequently, for 30 minutes, or until golden brown and cooked through, brushing with lemon mixture during cooking.

Note: Serve drumsticks as picnic fare or party nibbles with plenty of paper napkins for sticky fingers!

Serves 2

thigh
steaks with fruity mint salsa

Photograph page 23

ingredients

500g/I lb chicken thighs
Canola oil spray
salt, pepper to taste (optional)
¹/₂ teaspoon dried oregano
I pear, peeled and diced
I banana, peeled and diced
2 tablespoons lemon juice
3 tablespoons finely chopped mint
2 teaspoons sweet chilli sauce

Method:

1 Pound thigh fillets on both sides with a meat mallet to flatten. Sprinkle with salt (if using), pepper and oregano.

2 Heat a non-stick frying pan and lightly spray with oil, place in the thigh steaks and cook for 3 minutes on each side. Remove to a heated plate and keep hot. Add diced pear, banana, lemon juice, mint and chilli sauce to the pan. Scrape up pan juices and stir to heat fruit.

3 Pile hot fruit salsa on top of thigh steaks. Serve immediately with mashed potatoes or rice.

Serves 3-4

italian
pork in lemon sauce

Method:

1 Place flour, ¹/₂ teaspoon oregano and black pepper to taste in a shallow dish and mix to combine. Place egg, water and black pepper to taste in a separate shallow dish and whisk to combine. Place breadcrumbs and remaining oregano in a third shallow dish and mix to combine.

2 Coat pork with flour mixture, then dip in egg mixture and finally coat with breadcrumb mixture. Place coated pork on a plate lined with plastic food wrap and chill for 10-15 minutes.

3 Heat 2-3 tablespoons oil in a frying pan over a medium-high heat and cook 1-2 schnitzels (escalopes) at a time for 3 minutes each side or cook steaks for 4 minutes each side. Remove pork from pan, set aside and keep warm.

4 To make sauce, melt butter in same pan, then stir in lemon juice. Spoon sauce over pork and serve immediately.

Note: When cooking the pork it is important not to crowd the pan or the meat will steam and the coating will be soggy.

ingredients

flour
1 teaspoon dried oregano
freshly ground black pepper
1 egg, beaten
1 tablespoon cold water
dried breadcrumbs
8 pork schnitzels (escalopes) or
4 butterfly pork steaks, lightly pounded
vegetable oil

<u>Lemon butter sauce</u>
2 teaspoons butter
1 tablespoon lemon juice

This is also a delicious way of cooking chicken. In place of the pork use boneless chicken breast fillets. Pound the fillets lightly to flatten, then proceed as directed in the recipe. The cooking time for chicken will be 4 minutes each side.

Serves 4

Method:

1 Place beef, breadcrumbs, Parmesan cheese, oregano, ground garlic, eggs and black pepper to taste in a bowl and mix to combine. Form mixture into sixteen balls.

2 Heat oil in a frying pan over a medium heat, add meatballs and cook, turning frequently, for 10 minutes or until brown on all sides. Remove meatballs from pan and set aside.

3 Add red pepper (capsicum), onion and garlic to same pan and cook, stirring, for 3 minutes. Add mushrooms and cook for 4 minutes longer. Stir in pasta sauce, return meatballs to pan, cover and bring to simmering. Simmer, stirring occasionally, for 10 minutes.

Note: Serve spooned over hot spaghetti or pasta of your choice. This dish can be made 1-2 days in advance and reheated in the microwave when required. Dried ground garlic also called garlic powder can be found in the spice section of supermarkets. It has a pungent taste and smell and should be used with care.

Serves 6

italian
meatballs

ingredients

500g/1 lb lean beef mince
¹/₂ cup/60g/2oz dried breadcrumbs
2 tablespoons grated Parmesan cheese
1 teaspoon dried oregano
¹/₂ teaspoon dried ground garlic
2 eggs, beaten
freshly ground black pepper
1 tablespoon olive oil
1 red pepper (capsicum), diced
1 onion, diced
3 large cloves garlic, crushed
8 mushrooms, chopped
500g/16oz bottled tomato pasta sauce

vegetable
cheesecake

Method:

1 Place spinach in a sieve and squeeze to remove as much liquid as possible.
2 Place cream cheese, feta cheese, eggs, zucchini (courgettes), carrot, red pepper, spinach and black pepper to taste in a bowl and mix to combine.
3 Pour egg mixture into a greased 23cm/9in square cake tin, sprinkle with tasty cheese (mature cheddar) and bake for 25 minutes or until set.

Serving suggestion: Serve with wholegrain rolls and a salad of mixed lettuces and chopped fresh herbs. Also delicious cold this cheesecake is a tasty addition to any picnic and leftovers are always welcome in packed lunches.

Serves 4

ingredients

375g/12oz frozen spinach, thawed
250g/8oz cream cheese, softened
125g/4oz feta cheese, crumbled
4 eggs, lightly beaten
2 zucchini (courgettes), grated
1 carrot, grated
1 red pepper, chopped
freshly ground black pepper
60g/2oz tasty cheese (mature cheddar), grated

pesto
pasta

Method:

1 To make pesto, place basil leaves, parsley, Parmesan or Romano cheese, pine nuts or almonds, garlic and black pepper to taste in a food processor or blender and process to finely chop. With machine running, slowly add oil and continue processing to make a smooth paste.

2 Cook pasta in boiling water in a large saucepan following packet directions. Drain and divide between serving bowls, top with pesto, toss to combine and serve immediately.

Note: Spinach pesto makes a tasty alternative when fresh basil is unavailable. To make, use fresh spinach in place of the basil and add 1 teaspoon dried basil.

Serves 4

ingredients

500g/1 lb fettuccine or other pasta of your choice

Basil and garlic pesto
1 large bunch fresh basil
½ bunch fresh parsley, broken into sprigs
60g/2oz grated Parmesan or Romano cheese
30g/1oz pine nuts or almonds
2 large cloves garlic, quartered
freshly ground black pepper
⅓ cup/90mL/3fl oz olive oil

tandoori
beef burgers

Method:

1. To make dressing, place yoghurt, coriander, cumin and chilli powder to taste in a bowl and mix to combine. Cover and chill until required.
2. To make patties, place beef, garlic, breadcrumbs, egg, Tandoori paste and soy sauce in a bowl and mix to combine. Divide beef mixture into four portions and shape into patties.
3. Heat a little oil in a frying pan over a medium-high heat, add patties and cook for 4-5 minutes each side or until cooked to your liking.
4. Top bottom half of each roll with a lettuce leaf, some tomato slices, 2 cucumber slices, a pattie and a spoonful of dressing. Place other halves on top.

Note: These burgers are also delicious made using lamb mince in place of beef.

Serves 4

ingredients

4 wholemeal bread rolls, split and toasted
4 lettuce leaves
2 tomatoes, sliced
8 slices cucumber

Tandoori patties
500g/1 lb lean beef mince
2 cloves garlic, crushed
2 tablespoons dried breadcrumbs
1 egg
1¹⁄₂ tablespoons Tandoori paste
1 tablespoon soy sauce
vegetable oil

Spiced yoghurt dressing
¹⁄₂ cup/100g/3¹⁄₂oz natural yoghurt
1 tablespoon chopped fresh coriander
¹⁄₂ teaspoon ground cumin
pinch chilli powder

quick
chicken satay

Method:

1 Place oil, soy sauce, garlic and ginger in a bowl and mix to combine. Add chicken and marinate for 15 minutes.

2 Drain chicken, thread onto lightly oiled skewers and cook under a preheated medium grill or on a barbecue for 15-20 minutes or until chicken is cooked.

3 To make sauce, heat oil in a saucepan over a medium heat, add garlic and ginger and cook, stirring, for 2 minutes. Stir in stock, coconut milk and soy sauce, bring to simmering and simmer for 5 minutes.

4 Add peanut butter and simmer for 5 minutes longer. Just prior to serving, stir in chilli sauce. Serve sauce with chicken.

Note: The sauce can be made in advance and stored in a sealed container in the refrigerator for 5-7 days. Reheat over a low heat before serving. If sweet chilli sauce is not available mix ordinary chilli sauce with a little brown sugar.

Serves 4

ingredients

1 tablespoon vegetable oil
1 tablespoon soy sauce
1 large clove garlic, crushed
$^1/_2$ teaspoon finely grated fresh ginger
500g/1 lb boneless chicken thigh or breast fillets, skinned and cut into 2$^1/_2$ cm/1 in cubes

<u>Satay sauce</u>
1 teaspoon vegetable oil
2 large cloves garlic, crushed
2 teaspoons finely grated fresh ginger
1 cup/250mL/8fl oz chicken stock
1 cup/250mL/8fl oz coconut milk
1 tablespoon soy sauce
2 tablespoons crunchy peanut butter
2 teaspoons sweet chilli sauce

lamb
and almond pilau

Method:

1 Heat olive and vegetable oils together in a large saucepan over a low heat, add onions and cook, stirring frequently, for 10 minutes or until onions are golden. Remove from pan and set aside.

2 Increase heat to high and cook lamb in batches for 4-5 minutes or until lamb is well browned. Remove lamb from pan and set aside.

3 Wash rice under cold running water until water runs clears. Drain well. Add rice to pan and cook, stirring constantly, for 5 minutes. Slowly stir boiling stock into pan. Add thyme, oregano and black pepper to taste, then reduce heat, cover pan with a tight-fitting lid and simmer for 20 minutes or until all liquid is absorbed. Return lamb and onions to pan, cover and cook for 5 minutes longer.

4 Remove pan from heat and using a fork fluff up rice mixture. Sprinkle with raisins and almonds and serve.

Note: When cooking pilau it is important that the lid fits tightly on the pan. If the lid does not fit the pan tightly, first cover with aluminium foil, then with the lid.

Serves 6

ingredients

2 tablespoons olive oil
2 tablespoons vegetable oil
3 onions, quartered
500g/1 lb lean diced lamb
1 cup/220g/7oz long-grain rice
**3 cups/750mL/1¼ pt boiling
chicken or beef stock**
1 teaspoon dried thyme
1 teaspoon dried oregano
freshly ground black pepper
125g/4oz raisins
60g/2oz whole almonds, roasted

mongolian lamb

Photograph page 33

Method:

1 To make sauce, place cornflour in a small bowl, then stir in soy sauce, oyster sauce and stock. Set aside.
2 Heat oil in a wok or frying pan over a medium heat, add lamb and stir-fry for 3-4 minutes or until it just changes colour. Remove lamb from pan and set aside.
3 Add onions to pan and stir-fry for 2-3 minutes. Add spring onions, garlic and chillies and stir-fry for 2 minutes.
4 Return lamb to pan, add sauce and cook, stirring, for 2-3 minutes or until mixture thickens slightly. Sprinkle with coriander and serve immediately.

Note: When handling fresh chillies do not put your hands near your eyes or allow them to touch your lips. To avoid discomfort you might like to wear rubber gloves. Bottled minced chillies, available from supermarkets and Oriental food shops, are a convenient product that can be substituted for fresh chillies.

Serves 4

ingredients

2 tablespoons vegetable oil
500g/1 lb lamb fillet, cut into paper-thin slices
2 onions, cut into 8 wedges
4 spring onions, chopped
3 cloves garlic, crushed
2 small fresh red chillies, seeded and chopped
1 tablespoon chopped fresh coriander

Mongolian sauce
2¹/₂ teaspoons cornflour
1¹/₂ tablespoons light soy sauce
1 tablespoon oyster sauce
¹/₂ cup/125mL/4fl oz chicken stock

chinese
pork and spring onions

Photograph page 33

Method:

1 Using a sharp knife, cut pork across the grain into 5mm/¹/₄in thick slices. Place pork between sheets of greaseproof paper and pound lightly to tenderise and flatten.
2 To make marinade, place cornflour, garlic, soy sauce and sugar in a bowl and mix to combine. Add pork, toss to coat and marinate at room temperature for 20 minutes.
3 Heat oil in a wok or frying pan over a high heat, add pork and stir-fry for 5 minutes or until pork is tender.
4 Add spring onions, chilli, soy sauce and sherry and stir-fry for 1-2 minutes. Serve immediately.

Note: For a complete meal accompany with steamed vegetables of your choice and boiled rice or Oriental noodles.

Serves 4

ingredients

500g/1 lb pork fillet
3 tablespoons vegetable oil
4 spring onions, thinly sliced
1 red chilli, seeded and diced
1 tablespoon soy sauce
1 teaspoon sherry

Marinade
1 tablespoon cornflour
2 cloves garlic, crushed
1 tablespoon soy sauce
2 teaspoons sugar

*snapper with lemon
and coriander*

fast
food
from the barbecue

Quick cooking on the barbecue to feed

family and friends involves easy preparation with the many new sauces and marinades available today. Food in this chapter are all cooked over direct heat and take 4-16 mins to cook on flat-top barbecues, chargrills or on a hot-plate.

barbecue
lemon sardines

Method:

1 Place sardines in a bowl with salt and black pepper to taste. Add lemon juice and oil and lightly mix to coat. Set aside to marinate for 30 minutes.

2 Drain and roll sardines in breadcrumbs, pressing firmly to coat. Place on a piece of greased aluminium foil on the grill rack or hotplate over hot coals and cook for 2-3 minutes on each side, or until cooked through and golden. Sprinkle with parsley and serve immediately with lemon quarters.

Note: Look for small sardines about 10cm/4in long and cook them whole. If using larger fish, remove the heads, slit the stomach and remove entrails before cooking.

Serves 4

ingredients

**24 fresh sardines, cleaned
salt
freshly ground black pepper
3 tablespoons lemon juice
60ml/2fl oz vegetable or olive oil
60g/2oz breadcrumbs, made from stale bread
chopped fresh parsley for garnish
3 lemons, quartered to serve**

snapper fillets
with lemon and coriander

Photograph page 35

Method:

1 Mix the first 5 ingredients together in a shallow dish. Place the fillets in the dish and turn to coat well. Cover and stand 10-15 minutes.

2 Heat the barbecue to medium/hot and oil the grill bars. Place a sheet of baking paper over the bars and make a few slashes between the grill bars to allow ventilation. Place the fish on the paper and cook for 3-4 minutes each side according to thickness. Brush with marinade during cooking. Remove to plate. Heat any remaining marinade and pour over the fish.

Tip: Fish is cooked, if when tested with a fork, it flakes or the sections pull away. Lingfish, Haddock and Perch may also be used.

Serves 4

ingredients

**1 teaspoon chopped fresh ginger
1 teaspoon crushed garlic
2 tablespoons finely chopped coriander
2 tablespoon olive oil
1 1/2 tablespoon lemon juice
500g/1lb snapper fillets (4 portions)**

perfect
t-bone steak

Method:

1. Bring the steaks to room temperate. Mix garlic, oil and salt and pepper together. Rub onto both sides of the steak. Stand for 10-15 minutes at room temperature.

2. Heat the barbecue until hot and oil the grill bars. Arrange the steaks and sear for one minute each side. Move steaks to cooler part of the barbecue to continue cooking over moderate heat, or turn heat down. If heat cannot be reduced then elevate on a wire cake-rack placed on the grill bars. Cook until desired level is achieved. Total time 5-6 minutes for rare, 7-10 minutes for medium and 10-14 minutes for well done. Turn during cooking.

3. Serve on a heated steak plate and top with a dollop of garlic butter. Serve with jacket potatoes.

   Note: Many a time this delicious steak has been ruined on the barbecue.
   Cook on all barbecues and improvise a hood if using a flat-top barbecue.

Serves 4

ingredients

4 T-bone steaks
2 teaspoons crushed garlic
2 teaspoons oil
salt and pepper

Garlic Butter
60g/2oz butter
1 teaspoon crushed garlic
1 tablespoon parsley flakes
2 teaspoons lemon juice
mix all ingredients together and serve in a pot with a spoon

skewered
chicken liver in coriander

Method:

1 Place coriander, crushed garlic, chopped ginger oil and lemon juice in a bowl. Cut chicken livers into 2 through centre membrane and carefully stir into the coriander marinade. Cover and refrigerate for 1 hour or more.

2 Cut each bacon strip into 3 approximately 10cm/4in strips. Wrap a strip of bacon around each halved liver and secure with a toothpick.

3 Heat the barbecue until hot. Place on overturned wire cake-rack over the grill bars. Arrange the skewered livers on the rack. Cook for 8-10 minutes, turning frequently and brushing with any remaining marinade. Serve as finger food.

Note: Cook on any flat-top barbecue or electric barbecue grill.

**Yields approximately
22 skewers**

ingredients

**2 finely chopped coriander
1 teaspoon crushed garlic
1 teaspoon chopped
fresh ginger
2 teaspoons oil
1 tablespoon lemon juice
250g/8oz chicken livers
6 rashers bacon
toothpicks**

cajun
cutlets

Method:

1 Beat the butter to soften and mix in 1½ teaspoons of the cajun seasoning and the chopped chilli. Place butter along the centre of a piece of plastic wrap or greaseproof paper to one centimetre thickness. Fold plastic wrap over the butter then roll up. Smooth into a sausage shape and twist ends. Refrigerate to firm.

2 Trim the cutlets if necessary and snip the membrane at the side to prevent curling. Flatten slightly with the side of a meat mallet. Mix together 1½ teaspoons of the Cajun Seasoning and olive oil then rub mixture well into both sides of the cutlets. Place in a single layer onto a tray, cover and stand 20 minutes at room temperature, or longer in the refrigerator.

3 Heat the barbecue or electric barbecue grill to high. Place a sheet of baking paper on the grill bars, making a few slashes between the bars for ventilation. Place cutlets on grill and cook for 3 minutes each side for medium and 4 minutes for well-done. When cooked, transfer to a serving plate and top each cutlet with a round slice of Cajun butter. Serve immediately with vegetable accompaniments.

Note: Suitable for all barbecues. Ideal for electric grill/barbecue.

ingredients

125g/4oz butter
3 teaspoons Cajun seasoning
1 small red chilli, seeded and chopped
12 lamb cutlets
1 tablespoon olive oil

skewered
garlic prawns (shrimp)

Method:

1 Place soy sauce, oil, lemon juice, onion and garlic in a large deep bowl and mix well. Add prawns (shrimp), turning to coat in mixture, and marinate for at least 2 hours.
2 Drain prawns (shrimp), reserving marinade. Thread onto pre-soaked bamboo skewers alternately with spring onions and little sprigs of herbs. Cook over hot coals, brushing often with marinade, for 5-6 minutes, depending on size of prawns, or until tender.

Serves 4

ingredients

125ml/4fl oz light soy sauce
125ml/4fl oz vegetable oil
125ml/4fl oz lemon juice
1 small onion, finely chopped
3 cloves garlic, chopped
1kg/2lb uncooked prawns (shrimp), shelled and deveined, tails left intact
6 spring onions, cut into 2¹/₂cm/1in lengths
fresh oregano or thyme sprigs

teriyaki
prawns (shrimp)

Method:

1 Shell and devein prawns, leaving tail shells intact, or leave them in their shells, split each down the back and remove the vein. Place prawns (shrimp) in a deep bowl.
2 To make marinade, place soy sauce, oil, garlic, ginger, orange rind, sherry and brandy in a bowl, mix well and pour over prawns. Set aside to marinate for 2-3 hours, turning prawns occasionally.
3 Thread prawns (shrimp) onto pre-soaked bamboo skewers and cook over hot coals for 3-5 minutes or until they turn red and shells are opaque and crispy. Serve with remaining marinade for dipping.

Note: Prawns (shrimp) grilled in the shell untilthey turn crunchy are wonderful eaten shell and all. Provide finger bowls and plenty of paper napkins.

Serves 4

ingredients

750g/1¹/₂lb uncooked prawns (shrimp)

Ginger Sherry Marinade
125ml/4fl oz light soy sauce
60ml/2fl oz peanut oil
2 cloves garlic, crushed
2 tablespoons grated fresh ginger
small strip orange rind, finely shredded
2 tablespoons dry sherry
2 tablespoons brandy

barbecued
lamb pitta breads

Method:

1 Combine lemon rind, cumin and oil. Rub surface of lamb with oil mixture. Place in a shallow glass or ceramic dish and marinate at room temperature for 30 minutes.

2 Preheat barbecue to a medium heat. Place lamb on lightly oiled barbecue grill and cook for 3-5 minutes each side or until lamb is tender and cooked to your liking.

3 Warm pitta breads on barbecue for 1-2 minutes each side. Split each pitta bread to make pocket, then spread with hummus and fill with endive, tabbouleh and sliced lamb.

Note: For extra flavour serve with a spoonful of your favourite chutney.

Serves 6

ingredients

1 tablespoon finely grated lemon rind
1 teaspoon ground cumin
1 tablespoon olive oil
750g/1½lb lamb fillets
6 pitta bread rounds
6 tablespoons ready made hummus
1 bunch curly endive
250g/8oz ready-made tabbouleh

toasted
steak sandwiches

Method:

1 Cut the topside steak into 4 or 5 pieces and pound with a meat mallet until thin. Place in a non-metal container. Mix the lemon juice, garlic, salt, pepper and oil together and pour over the steaks. Turn to coat both sides and marinate for 30 minutes at room temperature, or longer in the refrigerator.

2 Soften the butter and spread a thin coating on both sides of the bread. If desired mix a little garlic into the butter.

3 Heat barbecue until hot and oil the grill bars and hotplate. Place onions on the hotplate. Toss and drizzle with a little oil as they cook. When beginning to soften, push to one side and turn occasionally with tongs. Place toast on hotplate and cook until golden on both sides. Place steaks on grill bars and cook 2 minutes on each side.

4 Assemble sandwiches as food cooks by placing steak and onions on one slice of toast, topping with a good squirt of steak sauce and closing with second slice of toast.

Note: A great favourite for backyard barbecue gatherings or fun family meals. Flat-top barbecues, hot-plates or kettle barbecues are best. May also be cooked on electric barbecue grills. For each sandwich allow 90g/3oz of raw steak per serve.

Yields 5 sandwiches

ingredients

500g/1lb topside steak
2 tablespoons lemon juice
1 teaspoon crushed garlic
salt and pepper
1 tablespoon oil
butter for spreading
10 slices toasted bread
2 large onions, thinly sliced
1 tablespoon oil
steak sauce of choice

barbecued
chicken and mushroom patties

Method:

1 Place ground chicken meat in a large bowl and add remaining ingredients except oil. Mix well to combine ingredients, then knead a little with one hand to make the meat fine in texture. With wet hands, shape into 4 or 5 flat patties.

2 Heat barbecue or grill to medium-high. Spray grill bars or rack with a little oil and place on the patties. Cook for 8 minutes on each side or until cooked through. Patties are cooked when juices run clear after being pricked with a skewer.

Serve hot with vegetable accompaniments.

Note: For quick preparation place onion, parsley and mushrooms in a food processor and chop together. May be cooked on flat-top barbecue, electric table grill or conventional gas or electric grill.

ingredients

500g/1lb ground chicken meat
1/2 cup dried breadcrumbs
1 medium onion, chopped
1/2 teaspoon salt
1/2 teaspoon pepper
2 tablespoons lemon juice
2 tablespoons chopped parsley
1/2 cup finely chopped mushrooms
vegetable oil

chicken nut stir-fry

wok cooking

As the wok has become almost standard

in many Western kitchens, so its uses have changed. The recipes in this book reflect these changes and tempt the cook with a selection of interesting and exciting tastes.

indonesian
chilli beef

Method:
1 Place vermicelli in a bowl, pour over enough hot water to cover and soak for 10 minutes. Drain, set aside and keep warm.
2 Heat oil in a large frying pan or wok over a medium heat, add beef, onion, chilli, garlic and black pepper to taste and stir-fry for 5 minutes, or until beef is cooked through.
3 Arrange vermicelli on serving plates and sprinkle with cucumber. Spoon meat over cucumber, sprinkle with peanuts and serve.
Note: Rice vermicelli (or cellophane noodles) do not require cooking after soaking, as the soaking is sufficient to rehydrate and tenderise.
Serves 4

ingredients

200g/6¹/₂oz rice vermicelli
1 tablespoon peanut oil
250g/8oz rump steak, thinly sliced
1 onion, quartered
1 fresh red chilli, finely chopped
2 cloves garlic, crushed
freshly ground black pepper
¹/₂ cucumber, peeled, seeded and diced
45g/1¹/₂oz roasted peanuts

chicken
and nut stir-fry

Photograph page 45

Method:
1 To make sauce, place marmalade, stock and lime juice in a bowl and mix to combine. Set aside.
2 Heat oil in a wok over a medium heat, add onion and ginger and stir-fry for 3 minutes or until onion is golden. Increase heat to high, add chicken and stir-fry for 5 minutes or until chicken is brown. Remove chicken mixture from wok, set aside and keep warm.
3 Add pear to wok and stir-fry for 3 minutes or until golden. Return chicken mixture to wok, add sauce and stir-fry for 3 minutes or until sauce thickens slightly. Season to taste with black pepper. Scatter with nuts and coriander and serve immediately.
Note: This stir-fry can be made using other nut oils and nuts. You might like to try walnut oil and walnuts or almond oil and almonds. Nut oils are available from larger supermarkets and specialty delicatessens.
Serves 4

ingredients

1 tablespoon macadamia or vegetable oil
1 onion, cut into eighths
2 tablespoons finely grated fresh ginger
4 boneless chicken breast fillets, thinly sliced
1 pear, peeled, cored and cut into thick slices
freshly ground black pepper
60g/2oz macadamias or Brazil nuts, chopped
2 tablespoons fresh coriander leaves

Ginger lime sauce
1 tablespoon ginger lime marmalade
¹/₂ cup/125mL/4fl oz chicken stock
1 tablespoon lime juice

warm
thai lamb salad

Method:

1 To make dressing, place coriander, sugar, soy and chilli sauces, lime juice and fish sauce in a bowl and mix to combine. Set aside.
2 Arrange lettuce leaves and cucumber on a serving platter and set aside.
3 Heat oil in a wok over a high heat, add lamb and stir-fry for 2 minutes or until brown. Place lamb on top of lettuce leaves, drizzle with dressing and serve immediately.

Note: This salad is also delicious made with pork fillet. Use a vegetable peeler to make long thin slices of cucumber - simply peel off lengthwise strips.

Serves 4

ingredients

250g/8oz assorted lettuce leaves
1 cucumber, sliced lengthwise into thin strips
2 teaspoons vegetable oil
500g/1 lb lamb fillets, trimmed of all visible fat, thinly sliced

Coriander and chilli dressing
2 tablespoons chopped fresh coriander
1 tablespoon brown sugar
$^1/_4$ cup/60mL/2fl oz soy sauce
2 tablespoons sweet chilli sauce
2 tablespoons lime juice
2 teaspoons fish sauce

wilted
arugula (rocket) cheese salad

Method:

1 Heat 2 tablespoons oil in a wok over a medium heat, add bread and stir-fry for 3 minutes or until golden. Drain on absorbent kitchen paper.

2 Heat remaining oil in wok, add spring onions and garlic and stir-fry for 2 minutes. Add zucchini (courgettes), red pepper (capsicum) and raisins and stir-fry for 3 minutes or until vegetables are just tender. Remove from wok and set aside.

3 Add arugula (rocket) to wok and stir-fry for 2 minutes or until rocket just wilts. Place arugula (rocket) on a serving platter or divide between individual bowls or plates, top with vegetable mixture and scatter with croûtons and blue cheese. Drizzle with balsamic vinegar and serve immediately.

Note: If arugula (rocket) is unavailable this salad is also delicious made with English spinach or watercress.

Serves 4

ingredients

3 tablespoons olive oil
4 slices white bread, crusts removed and cut into cubes
3 spring onions, sliced diagonally
2 cloves garlic, crushed
2 zucchini (courgettes), cut lengthwise into thin strips
1 red pepper (capsicum), thinly sliced
1/2 cup/90g/3oz raisins
2 bunches/250g/8oz arugula (rocket)
125g/4oz blue cheese, crumbled
2 tablespoons balsamic vinegar

bacon
and herb omelette

Method:

1 Heat oil in a wok over a medium heat, add leeks and bacon and stir-fry for 5 minutes or until bacon is crisp. Transfer leek mixture to a bowl, add parsley, basil and oregano and mix to combine. Set aside.

2 Place eggs, milk, cheese and black pepper to taste in a bowl and whisk to combine. Pour one-quarter of the egg mixture into wok and swirl so mixture covers base and sides. Top with one-quarter of the leek mixture and cook for 1 minute or until set. Remove from wok, roll up and place on a slice of toast. Repeat with remaining mixture to make 4 omelettes.

Note: Fresh mint can be used in place of the oregano if you wish. For a vegetarian version omit the bacon and replace with well-drained cooked spinach. Squeeze as much moisture as possible from the spinach before making the omelette.

Serves 4

ingredients

2 teaspoons vegetable oil
2 leeks, chopped
6 rashers bacon, chopped
2 tablespoons chopped fresh parsley
2 tablespoons chopped fresh basil
2 tablespoons chopped fresh oregano
6 eggs, lightly beaten
1/2 cup/125mL/4fl oz milk
60g/2oz grated tasty cheese (mature Cheddar)
freshly ground black pepper
4 thick slices wholemeal or grain bread, toasted

balsamic
pork stir-fry

Method:

1 Heat oil in a wok over a high heat, add garlic and stir-fry for 1 minute or until golden. Add pork and stir-fry for 3 minutes or until brown. Add red pepper (capsicum), green pepper (capsicum), orange juice and vinegar and stir-fry for 3 minutes or until pork is cooked. Season to taste with black pepper.

2 Divide rocket or watercress between serving plates, then top with pork mixture. Serve immediately.

Note: Balsamic vinegar is a dark red wine vinegar. Once a delicatessen item, in recent years it has become increasingly popular and can now be purchased from many supermarkets.

Serves 4

ingredients

2 teaspoons olive oil
2 cloves garlic, crushed
500g/1 lb pork fillet, trimmed of all visible fat, cut into 1cm/^{1}/$_2$in thick slices
1 red pepper (capsicum), chopped
1 green pepper (capsicum), chopped
^{1}/$_2$ cup/125mL/4fl oz orange juice
^{1}/$_4$ cup/60mL/2fl oz balsamic vinegar
freshly ground black pepper
1 bunch/125g/4oz rocket or watercress leaves

plum
and chilli beef stir fry

Method:

1 Trim beef of any excess fat. Slice into thin strips across the grain. Put large saucepan of water on to boil for noodles.
2 Heat oil in a wok of frypan. Stir fry garlic and onion 1 minute. Add beef in two batches, stir fry 2-3 minutes. Add zucchini (courgette) and capsicum (pepper) stir fry 2 minutes.
3 Add combined ground ginger, chilli sauce, plum sauce and cornflour to beef vegetables and corn. Cook 2-3 minutes.
4 Meanwhile, cook noodles in boiling water 2-3 minutes.
5 Serve beef stir fry with noodles

Serves 4-6

ingredients

750g/1 ½lb lean steak
2 teaspoons olive oil
2 teaspoons freshly crushed garlic
1 onion, cut in wedges, petals separated
1 large zucchini (courgette),
sliced diagonally
1 red capsicum (pepper), cut into
2½cm/1in cubes
¼ teaspoon ground ginger
1-2 teaspoons hot chilli sauce
½ cup plum sauce
2 teaspoons cornflour
440g/14oz can baby corn, drained
375g/12oz rice noodles

stir-fry
chilli prawns (shrimp)

Method:

1 Heat vegetable and sesame oils together in a wok over a medium heat, add garlic and chillies and stir-fry for 1 minute. Add prawns (shrimp) and stir-fry for 2 minutes or until they change colour.

2 Stir in sugar, tomato juice and soy sauce and stir-fry, for 3 minutes or until sauce is heated through.

Note: For a complete meal, serve prawns (shrimp) with boiled rice or noodles of your choice and stir-fried vegetables.

Serves 4

ingredients

1 teaspoon vegetable oil
1 teaspoon sesame oil
3 cloves garlic, crushed
3 fresh red chillies, chopped
1 kg/2 lb uncooked medium prawns (shrimp), shelled and deveined
1 tablespoon brown sugar
1/3 cup/90mL/3fl oz tomato juice
1 tablespoon soy sauce

stir-fry
lime wings

Method:
1 Place chicken wings in a flat non-metal container. Combine lime juice, vinegar, sugar and soy sauce and pour over the wings, turn into coat. Marinate for 30 minutes or longer.
2 Heat the wok, add oil and heat. Remove wings from marinade and stir-fry about 15 minutes until brown and tender. Add shallots and stir-fry one minute then pour in the marinade. Stir to coat and heat through. Remove to a platter.
3 Add the lime slices and water to the wok. Allow to simmer to tenderise the slices. Stir in the sugar and vinegar and cook until the slices are coated with a thick syrup. Remove and arrange over and between the wings. Pour over any remaining syrup. Serve as finger food or as a meal with rice and vegetables.
Yields 12 pieces

ingredients

1kg/2lb chicken wings, tips removed
1/4 cup lime juice
1 tablespoon white wine vinegar
2 tablespoons brown sugar
2 teaspoons soy sauce

Soy sauce
2 tablespoons canola oil
1/4 cup sliced shallots

Garnish
2 limes, thinly sliced
1/2 cup water
1/4 cup white sugar
1/2 teaspoon white wine vinegar

*fish fillets with yoghurt
marinade*

microwave
cooking

In this chapter you will find recipes

*that save you time and dishes that are every bit
as good as if they were cooked conventionally – in
fact most are better. It is also all about showing
you how to make the most of your microwave and
use it to its full potential.*

couscous
marrakesh

Method:
1 Place couscous in a microwavable bowl, pour over stock and toss with a fork. Cover and stand for 5 minutes or until liquid is absorbed.
2 Place spring onions and oil in a separate microwavable bowl, cover with a microwavable plate and set aside.
3 Place squash or zucchini (courgettes) in a clean microwavable plastic bag. Twist neck of bag and fold under vegetables to seal. Place bag on plate on top of bowl and cook on High (100%) for 5 minutes.
4 Add spring onions, squash or zucchini (courgettes), prunes, nuts, orange rind and orange juice to couscous and mix to combine. Cover and cook on Medium (50%) for 4 minutes or until heated through.
Note: The microwave is handy for heating savoury couscous dishes through before serving ensuring they are hot, but not dry or burnt. Serve with a lamb or chicken casserole, roast meat or as a vegetable dish for a vegetarian meal.
Serves 4

ingredients

1 cup/185g/6oz couscous
1 cup/250mL/8fl oz boiling chicken or vegetable stock, made with stock cubes
3 spring onions, sliced
1 tablespoon olive oil
125g/4oz yellow squash, cut into wedges or zucchini (courgettes), sliced
12 dessert prunes, pitted and quartered
60g/2oz pistachio nuts, coarsely chopped
2 teaspoons finely grated orange rind
2 tablespoons orange juice

fish
fillets with yoghurt marinade

Photograph page 55

Method:
1 To make marinade, place yoghurt, chilli sauce, coriander and chilli in a bowl and mix to combine. Place fish fillets in a shallow glass or ceramic dish, spoon over marinade, cover and marinate in the refrigerator for at least 3 hours.
2 Place fish in a shallow microwavable dish, with thickest parts of fillets towards edge of dish. Spoon over any remaining marinade, cover and cook on Medium (50%) for 4 minutes. To serve, place fillets on serving plates, stir sauce and spoon over fish.
Note: Delicious served with savoury couscous, snow peas (mangetout) and carrots.
Serves 2

ingredients

2 fillets cod or similar fish, skinned

Yoghurt chilli marinade
²/₃ cup/140g/4¹/₂oz natural yoghurt
2 tablespoons sweet chilli sauce
2 tablespoons chopped fresh coriander
1 fresh red chilli, seeded and finely chopped

tandoori
prawn (shrimp) rolls

Method:

1 Place tandoori paste and 1 tablespoon yoghurt in a bowl and mix to combine. Add prawns (shrimp0 and toss to coat. Cover and marinate in the refrigerator for at least 1 hour or up to 24 hours.

2 Place prawns (shrimp, like numbers on a clock face with the thickest part towards the edge, on a microw dinner plate and cook on High (100%) for 1 minute, then on Medium (50%) for 1-2 minutes or until prawns (shrimp) change colour and are cooked.

3 Heat naan bread on Defrost (30%) for 1 minute. Place 6 prawns (shrimp) along centre of each naan bread, top with cucumber and 2 tablespoons yoghurt, roll up and serve immediately.

Note: A delicious snack, perfect for a weekend lunch or supper on the run. The longer you marinate the prawns (shrimp) the more robust the flavour. Take care not to overcook the prawns (shrimp) or they will become tough.

ingredients

3 tablespoons tandoori paste
natural yoghurt
12 large uncooked prawns (shrimp),
shelled and deveined
2 naan bread
4 tablespoons coarsely chopped
cucumber

peanut
beef curry

Method:

1 Place oil, onion, garlic and chilli in a microwavable casserole dish, cover and cook on High (100%) for 3 minutes.
2 Stir in beef, satay sauce, coconut milk and lemon juice, cover and cook for 5 minutes.
3 Add green beans and red pepper (capsicum), stir, cover and cook on Medium (50%) for 5 minutes or until vegetables are tender crisp.

Note: For a complete meal serve with brown or white rice or Oriental noodles.

Serves 4

ingredients

1 tablespoon peanut (groundnut) oil
1 onion, finely chopped
2 cloves garlic, crushed
1 teaspoon finely chopped fresh red chilli
500g/1 lb rump steak or silverside,
cut into thin strips
220g/7oz bottled satay stir-fry sauce
1/2 cup/125mL/4fl oz coconut milk
2 tablespoons lemon juice
250g/8oz green beans, halved
1 red pepper (capsicum), thinly sliced

veal
cacciatore

Method:

1 *Place eggplant (aubergine), garlic and dressing in a bowl and mix to combine.*

2 *Place veal around edge of a microwavable casserole dish and place eggplant (aubergine) in the centre, cover and cook on High (100%) for 3 minutes.*

3 *Stir in sauce, cover and cook on Medium (50%) for 5 minutes, stir, then cook for 5 minutes longer or until veal is cooked. Scatter with olives and serve immediately.*

Note: *This is a quick version of a classic recipe which uses a good quality processed sauce to save time. For a complete meal serve with pasta, noodles or rice and a tossed green salad.*

Serves 4

ingredients

1 eggplant (aubergine), cut into
1cm/¹/₂in cubes
1 clove garlic, crushed
¹/₃ cup/90mL/3fl oz French dressing
4 thin slices veal steak or schnitzel
(escalopes), cut into thin strips
500mL/16fl oz jar cacciatore or similar
tomato pasta sauce
8 green olives, sliced

hot
potato salad

Method:

1 Using a sharp knife score around the circumference of each potato.

2 Place potatoes evenly around edge of turntable and cook on High (100%) for 5 minutes, turn over and cook for 3-5 minutes longer or until potatoes are cooked. Set aside until cool enough to handle, then remove skin and cut potatoes into 1cm/1/2in cubes.

3 Place onion and bacon in a microwavable bowl, cover and cook on High (100%) for 3 minutes, stir, then cook for 2 minutes longer.

4 Stir in cornflour, stock and vinegar, cover and cook for 4 minutes. Add mustard, cream and potatoes and mix gently to combine. Cover and cook on Medium (50%) for 2 minutes or until hot. Season to taste with black pepper and sprinkle with chives. Serve warm.

Note: This is a good hot dish to serve at a salad buffet or barbecue. Flat oval-shaped potatoes seem to cook the most evenly in the microwave.

Serves 6

ingredients

4 red-skinned potatoes, about 750g/1½ lb
1 onion, diced
2 rashers bacon, chopped
2 tablespoons cornflour
1 cup/250mL/8fl oz vegetable stock
¼ cup/60mL/2fl oz cider or tarragon vinegar
2 tablespoons wholegrain mustard
⅓ cup/90mL/3fl oz cream (double)
freshly ground black pepper
snipped fresh chives

Method:

1 *To make stuffing, place butter and spring onions in a small microwavable bowl, cover with a piece of absorbent kitchen paper and cook on High (100%) for 2 minutes. Add spinach, breadcrumbs and black pepper to taste and mix to combine. Unroll loin and spread with stuffing. Reroll and tie securely with kitchen string.*

2 *To make glaze, place mustard, barbecue sauce and tomato sauce in a bowl, mix to combine and brush over lamb.*

3 *Heat a microwave browning dish on High (100%) for 3 minutes. Place lamb in centre of dish and roll to brown outside and to seal. Cook on HIGH (100%) for 3 minutes, then on Medium (50%) for 9 minutes. Alternatively, brown meat in a frying pan then transfer to a microwavable dish and cook as directed.*

4 *Cover lamb with aluminium foil and stand for 5 minutes.*

Note: *Select symetrically shaped joints without bones for even cooking and trim off as much fat as possible. A marinade or glaze helps to give the meat an appetising appearance. Serve lamb with mint jelly or sauce, carrots and creamy mashed potatoes.*

Serves 2-3

stuffed
loin of lamb

ingredients

500g/1 lb boned and rolled loin of lamb, trimmed of all visible fat

Spinach stuffing
15g/¹/₂oz butter
8 spring onions, thinly sliced
125g/4oz cooked spinach, well drained
1 slice wholemeal bread, crumbed
freshly ground black pepper

Mustard glaze
1 tablespoon wholegrain mustard
1 tablespoon barbecue sauce
1 tablespoon tomato sauce

chocolate
shortcake

Method:

1 Melt chocolate in a microwavable bowl on Defrost (30%) for 2 minutes, stir, then heat for 2 minutes longer. Continue in this way for 6-8 minutes longer or until chocolate is completely melted.

2 Stir shortbread into chocolate, then add sour cream or cream, almonds or hazelnuts and liqueur, if using, and mix well to combine.

3 Press mixture in a base-lined and buttered 18cm/7in diameter round cake tin and chill until firm.

Note: This is a quick and slick treat for chocoholics who don't want to spend a lot of time in the kitchen. Serve cut into wedges for morning coffee or afternoon tea or with sugared berries for a simple dessert.

Makes an 18cm/7in round cake

ingredients

200g/6¹/₂oz dark cooking chocolate, broken into small pieces
100g/3¹/₂oz shortbread finger biscuits, cut into chunky pieces
¹/₂ cup/125g/4oz sour cream or
¹/₂ cup/125mL/4fl oz cream (double)
¹/₂ cup/60g/2oz ground almonds or hazelnuts
1 tablespoon orange-flavoured or whiskey liqueur (optional)

rhubarb
and strawberry crumble

Method:

1 Place rhubarb into a microwavable dish, sprinkle with sugar, cover and cook on High (100%) for 3 minutes, stir, then cook for 2 minutes longer. Scatter strawberries over cooked rhubarb.

2 To make topping, place flour and butter in a food processor and process for 30 seconds or until mixture resembles fine breadcrumbs. Add muesli, wheat germ, burghul (cracked wheat) and nutmeg and using the pulse process briefly to combine.

3 Sprinkle topping over fruit and cook on Medium (50%) for 5 minutes.

Note: Stewed rhubarb and fresh strawberries are a delicious and colourful combination in this superb dessert. Serve crumble hot with thick cream, vanilla ice cream or mascarpone.

Serves 6

ingredients

500g/1 lb rhubarb, trimmed and pink parts only cut into ¹/₂cm/1in pieces
¹/₄ cup/45g/1¹/₂oz brown sugar
250g/8oz strawberries, quartered or halved

Muesli crumble topping
¹/₂ cup/75g/2¹/₂oz wholemeal flour
60g/2oz unsalted butter, cubed
¹/₂ cup/100g/3¹/₂oz toasted muesli
1 tablespoon wheat germ
1 tablespoon burghul (cracked wheat)
¹/₂ teaspoon ground nutmeg

microwave
essentials

The microwave is great for all those little jobs that are time consuming when done conventionally. Use these hints and tips to make the most of your microwave and to save time when preparing meals.

Jam or honey:
Melt for use in cooking. Remove lid from jar. Place jar in microwave and cook on HIGH (100%) for 20-30 seconds or until melted. The jam or honey can now be easily measured.

Ice cream:
To soften hard ice cream for serving, place ice cream container in microwave and cook on MEDIUM (50%) for 1 minute. Remove from microwave and allow to stand for a few minutes before removing scoops.

Butter or cream cheese:
To soften butter or cream cheese, cook on DEFROST (30%) for 40-60 seconds.

Pastry Cream and Hollandaise Sauce:
Egg-based sauces are easy to make in the microwave. Cook on MEDIUM (50%), stirring frequently during cooking until sauce thickens slightly. Remove sauce when cooking is almost complete. The sauce will finish cooking if you allow it to stand.

Stale bread:
Freshen stale bread by wrapping in absorbent kitchen paper and cooking on HIGH (100%) for 20-30 seconds.

Even cooking:
Arrange food so that the thicker portions are on the outside of turntable and thinner portions towards the centre. You will find that the food will cook more evenly.

Covering:
To cover or not to cover. Generally, food that requires covering for conventional cooking will also need to be covered for microwave cooking. Most food requires covering when reheating.

Defrosting:
Pack meat or chicken cuts in single layers to freeze. Thaw in the microwave on DEFROST (30%). Remove thawed cuts, then continue to microwave until remaining cuts are defrosted.

Instant Hot Dog:
Make three slashes across frankfurt and place in a buttered roll. Wrap roll in absorbent kitchen paper and cook on HIGH (100%) for 30 seconds.

Plump up dried fruits:
When cooking cakes and puddings use the microwave to plump up the fruit. For 500g dried fruit, place fruit in a large microwave-safe dish, add 1 cup (250 mL) water, cover and cook on HIGH (100%) for 3-4 minutes, or until fruit is no longer dried. Stir and set aside to stand for 30 minutes or until cool enough to complete recipe.

Melting chocolate:
Break chocolate into small pieces and place in a microwave-safe jug. Cook on HIGH (100%) for 1-2 minutes per 200g of chocolate. Stir frequently during cooking.

Plastic containers and plastic food wrap:
Only use containers and plastic food wraps marked microwave safe.

Peeling tomatoes:
Score skin of tomatoes with a sharp knife, then cook on HIGH (100%) for 10-15 seconds per tomato.

Microwaved vegetables:
Vegetables cooked in the microwave retain more of their colour and nutrients, because of the quicker cooking time and small quantity of water used.

Stale potato chips:
Revive these by placing on absorbent kitchen paper and cooking on HIGH (100%) for 30 seconds, set aside and allow to cool.

Speedy roast dinner:
To shorten the cooking time of a roast dinner but still achieve a crispy result, start the cooking in the microwave, then transfer to the oven to complete. For a 1.5 kg chicken, cook in the microwave on HIGH (100%) for 15 minutes, then bake in oven at 220°C for 30 minutes or until golden. For 8 potatoes, cook in the microwave on HIGH (100%) for 6 minutes, then bake in oven at 220°C for 20-30 minutes or until tender and crisp.

Juicier fruit:
Get more juice from your fruit by warming on HIGH (100%) for 30 seconds per piece of fruit. Set aside to stand for 5 minutes then squeeze.

Standing time:
Larger portions of food, such as whole chickens or roasts require standing time after cooking time is completed. For best results, cover with aluminium foil and stand for 10-15 minutes before slicing. This allows the juices to settle and the heat to equalise.

Quicker cooking:
Food that is at room temperature will cook faster than refrigerated foods. Lighter foods cook more rapidly than dense food; for example, potatoes and pumpkin will take longer to cook than broccoli or eggs.

Toasting of coconut and nuts:
This can be achieved quickly and efficiently in the microwave. For coconut, spread it over a microwave-safe dish and cook on HIGH (100%) for 5-6 minutes, stirring frequently during cooking until golden. Remember coconut can still burn in the microwave if overcooked. To toast nuts, place in a single layer in a microwave-safe dish and cook on HIGH (100%) for 5-6 minutes or until golden. Stir frequently during cooking to prevent burning.

rum raisin nut brownies

quick bakes

The aroma of a freshly baked cake,

the taste of a still warm biscuit and the compliments of family and friends is what quick bakes is all about. Baking has never been simpler, quicker or more fun than with this selection of easy cakes and bakes.

hazelnut
shortbread

Method:

1 Place butter, flour, hazelnuts and ground rice in a food processor and process until mixture resembles coarse breadcrumbs. Add sugar and process to combine.

2 Turn mixture onto a floured surface and knead lightly to make a pliable dough. Place dough between sheets of baking paper and roll out to 5mm/¹/₄in thick. Using a 5cm/2in fluted cutter, cut out rounds of dough and place 2¹/₂cm/1 in apart on greased baking trays. Bake for 20-25 minutes or until lightly browned. Stand on baking trays for 2-3 minutes before transferring to wire racks to cool.

3 Place melted chocolate in a plastic food bag, snip off one corner and pipe lines across each biscuit.

Note: The consistency of chopped or ground nuts is important to the success of a recipe. Ground nuts should be a powder not a paste. Particular care should be taken when using a food processor or grinder as they chop very quickly. When using a food processor use the pulse button and only chop about 60g/2oz at a time. This helps avoid overworking the nuts.

Makes 40

ingredients

250g/8oz butter, chopped
1¹/₂ cups/185g/6oz flour, sifted
45g/1¹/₂oz hazelnuts, ground
¹/₄ cup/45g/1¹/₂oz ground rice
¹/₄ cup/60g/2oz caster sugar
100g/3¹/₂oz chocolate, melted

Oven temperature 160°C/325°F/Gas 3

Oven temperature 180°C, 350°F, Gas 4

easy
banana loaf

Method:

1 Place butter, sugar, brown sugar, eggs, vanilla essence, lemon rind, flour and banana in a bowl and beat for 5 minutes or until mixture is light and smooth.

2 Pour mixture into a greased and lined 11x21cm/4¹/₂x8¹/₂in loaf tin and bake for 45 minutes or until loaf is cooked when tested with a skewer. Stand loaf in tin for 5 minutes before turning onto a wire rack to cool.

Note: When grating lemon or orange rind, take care not to grate the white pith beneath the skin as it has a bitter unpleasant taste. Grate the rind on a fine-textured grater or use a metal 'zester' tool which consists of a row of tiny holes that cuts and curls fine, long slivers of rind.

Makes an 11x21cm/4¹/₂x 8¹/₂in loaf

ingredients

250g/8oz butter, softened
¹/₂ cup/125g/4oz sugar
¹/₂ cup/90g/3oz brown sugar
3 eggs, lightly beaten
1 teaspoon vanilla essence
2 teaspoons finely grated lemon rind
2 cups/250g/8oz self-raising flour, sifted
2 ripe bananas, mashed

shaggy
dog lamingtons

Method:

1 Cut cake into 5cm/2in squares. Split each square horizontally and set aside.

2 To make filling, place cream and chocolate in a heatproof bowl set over a saucepan of simmering water and heat, stirring, until chocolate melts and mixture is smooth. Remove bowl from pan and set aside to cool. Beat filling until light and fluffy.

3 Spread filling over bottom half of cake squares and top with remaining cake squares.

4 To make icing, sift icing sugar and cocoa powder together in a bowl, add butter and mix to combine. Stir in enough milk to make an icing with a smooth coating consistency.

5 Dip cake squares in icing to coat completely. Roll in coconut and dust with drinking chocolate. Refrigerate until ready to serve.

Note: To make coating the cake easier, place coconut and icing in two shallow dishes or cake tins. Use tongs or two forks to dip the cake in the icing, then place on a wire rack set over a sheet of paper and allow to drain for 2-3 minutes before rolling in the coconut.

Makes 12

ingredients

1x18x28 cm/7x11in butter or sponge cake
185g/6oz shredded coconut
drinking chocolate, sifted

Chocolate cream filling
1¼ cups/315mL/10fl oz cream (double)
200g/6½oz dark chocolate, chopped

Chocolate icing
2 cups/315g/10oz icing sugar
2 tablespoons cocoa powder
30g/1oz butter, softened
¼ cup/60mL/2fl oz milk

apricot
oatmeal slice

Photograph page 73

ingredients

**2 cups/315g/10oz wholemeal flour
1 teaspoon bicarbonate soda
2¹/₂cups/235g/7¹/₂oz rolled oats
1 cup/170g/5¹/₂oz brown sugar
200g/6¹/₂oz butter, melted
icing sugar for dusting**

**<u>Apricot filling</u>
250g/8oz dried apricots
²/₃ cup/170mL/5¹/₂fl oz water
2 tablespoons apricot jam**

Method:

1 *To make filling, place apricots, water and jam in a saucepan and cook over a low heat, stirring, until jam melts. Bring to the boil, then reduce heat and simmer for 5 minutes or until mixture thickens. Remove from heat and set aside to cool.*

2 *Sift flour and bicarbonate of soda together in a bowl. Return husks to bowl. Add rolled oats, sugar and butter and mix well to combine.*

3 *Press half the oat mixture over the base of a greased and lined 18x28cm/7x11in shallow cake tin. Spread with filling and sprinkle with remaining oat mixture.*

4 *Bake for 35 minutes or until slice is cooked. Cool in tin, then cut into bars and sprinkle with icing sugar.*

Note: *This slice is delicious made using any dried fruit. For something different why not try dried dates or figs.*

Makes 28

Oven temperature 180°C, 350°F, Gas 4

peanut
butter cookies

Photograph page 73

ingredients

**250g/8oz butter, softened
1 cup/265g/8¹/₂oz peanut butter
1 cup/170g/5¹/₂oz brown sugar
2 eggs, lightly beaten
2¹/₄cups/280g/9oz flour, sifted
2 teaspoons bicarbonate of soda, sifted**

Method:

1 *Place butter, peanut butter and sugar in a bowl and beat until light and fluffy. Gradually beat in eggs.*

2 *Stir flour and bicarbonate of soda together. Add to egg mixture and mix well. Roll tablespoons of mixture into balls, place on lightly greased baking trays and flatten slightly.*

3 *Bake for 15 minutes or until cookies are golden and crisp. Stand on trays for 3 minutes before transferring to wire racks to cool.*

Note: *For a traditional look to these biscuits, flatten the dough balls with a fork so that the tines of the fork leave a chequerboard imprint.*

Makes 36

Oven temperature 180°C, 350°F, Gas 4

chocolate
cream hearts

Method:

1 Place butter, sugar and vanilla essence in a bowl and beat until light and fluffy. Add egg and beat well.

2 Sift together flour, cocoa powder and baking powder over butter mixture and fold in with milk.

3 Knead mixture lightly to form a ball, then wrap in plastic food wrap and refrigerate for 30 minutes. Roll out dough on a lightly floured surface to 3mm/^{1}/8in thick.

4 Using a heart-shaped cutter, cut out biscuits, place on greased baking trays and bake for 10 minutes. Transfer biscuits to wire racks to cool.

5 To make Chocolate Cream, place chocolate and butter in a heatproof bowl set over a saucepan of simmering water and heat, stirring constantly, until mixture is smooth. Remove bowl from pan and set aside to cool slightly.

6 Spread half the biscuits with Chocolate Cream and top with remaining biscuits.

Note: Decorate the top of these biscuits by piping crisscross lines of melted dark or white chocolate – or both!

Makes 20

ingredients

125g/4oz butter, softened
1 cup/250g/8oz sugar
1 teaspoon vanilla essence
1 egg, lightly beaten
2^1/2 cups/315g/10oz flour
^{1}/4 cup/30g/1oz cocoa powder
1^1/2 teaspoons baking powder
^{1}/2 cup/125mL/4fl oz milk

Chocolate cream
125g/4oz dark chocolate, chopped
100g/3^1/2oz butter

Oven temperature 180°C, 350°F, Gas 4

hazelnut
coconut slice

Method:

1 Place flour, sugar and butter in a food processor and process until mixture forms a soft dough.
2 Press dough into the base of a 20cm/8in square tin and bake for 10 minutes. Set aside to cool.
3 To make topping, combine hazelnuts, coconut, brown sugar and flour in a bowl. Add eggs and mix to combine.
4 Spread topping over base. Increase oven temperature to 190°C/375°F/Gas 5 and bake for 20 minutes longer or until topping is golden. Cool slice in tin, then cut into squares.

Note: Fat or shortening in whatever form makes a baked product tender and helps to improve its keeping quality. In most baked goods, top quality margarine and butter are interchangeable.

Makes 16

ingredients

1 cup/125g/4oz flour
¼ cup/60g/2oz sugar
100g/3½oz butter, softened

Nutty topping
155g/5oz hazelnuts, roughly chopped
45g/1½oz desiccated coconut
2 cups/350g/11oz brown sugar
¼ cup/30g/1oz flour
2 eggs, lightly beaten

Oven temperature 180°C/350°F/Gas 4

caramel
hazelnut cake

caramel hazelnut cake

ingredients
4 eggs
1 cup/220g/7oz caster sugar
1¼ cups/155g/5oz self-raising flour, sifted
⅓ cup/45g/1½oz ground hazelnuts
½ cup/125mL/4fl oz milk, warmed
15g/½oz butter, melted
60g/2oz whole hazelnuts

Caramel and cream filling
2 cups/500mL/16fl oz cream (double)
1 tablespoon icing sugar, sifted
375g/12oz soft caramels

Oven temperature 180°C, 350°F, Gas 4

Method:

1 Place eggs in a bowl and beat until thick and creamy. Gradually add caster sugar, beating well after each addition, until mixture is creamy.

2 Combine flour and ground hazelnuts. Fold flour mixture, milk and butter into egg mixture. Pour mixture into two greased and lined 20cm/8in round cake tins and bake for 25 minutes or until cakes are cooked when tested with a skewer. Turn onto wire racks to cool.

3 To make filling, place cream and icing sugar in a bowl and beat until thick. Place caramels in a saucepan and cook, stirring, over a low heat until caramels melt and mixture is smooth. Remove from heat and set aside to cool slightly.

4 To assemble, split each cake in half horizontally using a serrated edged knife. Place one layer of cake on a serving plate, spread with cream mixture, drizzle with caramel and top with a second layer of sponge. Repeat layers, finishing with a layer of filling and drizzling with caramel. Decorate top of cake with whole hazelnuts.

Note: Caramelised hazelnuts make an elegant garnish for this European-style dessert cake. To make, gently melt a little granulated sugar in a frying pan until it turns a pale golden colour. Remove from heat, quickly drop in whole toasted hazelnuts and stir briskly with a wooden spoon until well coated. Cool on an oiled baking sheet or on baking paper.

Makes a 20cm/8in round cake

Cooking is not an exact science: one does not require finely calibrated scales, pipettes and scientific equipment to cook, yet the conversion to metric measures in some countries and its interpretations must have intimidated many a good cook.

Weights are given in the recipes only for ingredients such as meats, fish, poultry and some vegetables. Though a few grams/ounces one way or another will not affect the success of your dish.

Though recipes have been tested using the Australian Standard 250mL cup, 20mL tablespoon and 5mL teaspoon, they will work just as well with the US and Canadian 8fl oz cup, or the UK 300mL cup. We have used graduated cup measures in preference to tablespoon measures so that proportions are always the same. Where tablespoon measures have been given, these are not crucial measures, so using the smaller tablespoon of the US or UK will not affect the recipe's success. At least we all agree on the teaspoon size.

For breads, cakes and pastries, the only area which might cause concern is where eggs are used, as proportions will then vary. If working with a 250mL or 300mL cup, use large eggs (60g/2oz), adding a little more liquid to the recipe for 300mL cup measures if it seems necessary. Use the medium-sized eggs (55g/1¼oz) with 8fl oz cup measure. A graduated set of measuring cups and spoons is recommended, the cups in particular for measuring dry ingredients. Remember to level such ingredients to ensure their accuracy.

English measures

All measurements are similar to Australian with two exceptions: the English cup measures 300mL/10fl oz, whereas the Australian cup measure 250mL/8fl oz. The English tablespoon (the Australian dessertspoon) measures 14.8mL/½fl oz against the Australian tablespoon of 20mL/¾fl oz.

American measures

The American reputed pint is 16fl oz, a quart is equal to 32fl oz and the American gallon, 128fl oz. The Imperial measurement is 20fl oz to the pint, 40fl oz a quart and 160fl oz one gallon.

The American tablespoon is equal to 14.8mL/½fl oz, the teaspoon is 5mL/⅙fl oz. The cup measure is 250mL/8fl oz, the same as Australia.

Dry measures

All the measures are level, so when you have filled a cup or spoon, level it off with the edge of a knife. The scale below is the "cook's equivalent"; it is not an exact conversion of metric to imperial measurement. To calculate the exact metric equivalent yourself, use 2.2046 lb = 1kg or 1 lb = 0.45359kg

Metric		Imperial	
g = grams		oz = ounces	
kg = kilograms		lb = pound	
15g		½oz	
20g		⅔oz	
30g		1oz	
60g		2oz	
90g		3oz	
125g		4oz	¼ lb
155g		5oz	
185g		6oz	
220g		7oz	
250g		8oz	½ lb
280g		9oz	
315g		10oz	
345g		11oz	
375g		12oz	¾ lb
410g		13oz	
440g		14oz	
470g		15oz	
1,000g	1kg	35.2oz	2.2 lb
	1.5kg		3.3 lb

Oven temperatures

The Celsius temperatures given here are not exact; they have been rounded off and are given as a guide only. Follow the manufacturer's temperature guide, relating it to oven description given in the recipe. Remember gas ovens are hottest at the top, electric ovens at the bottom and convection-fan forced ovens are usually even throughout. We included Regulo numbers for gas cookers which may assist. To convert °C to °F multiply °C by 9 and divide by 5 then add 32.

Oven temperatures

	C°	F°	Regulo
Very slow	120	250	1
Slow	150	300	2
Moderately slow	150	325	3
Moderate	180	350	4
Moderately hot	190-200	370-400	5-6
Hot	210-220	410-440	6-7
Very hot	230	450	8
Super hot	250-290	475-500	9-10

Cake dish sizes

Metric	Imperial
15cm	6in
18cm	7in
20cm	8in
23cm	9in

Loaf dish sizes

Metric	Imperial
23x12cm	9x5in
25x8cm	10x3in
28x18cm	11x7in

Liquid measures

Metric	Imperial	Cup & Spoon
mL	fl oz	
millilitres	fluid ounce	
5mL	$^1/_6$fl oz	1 teaspoon
20mL	$^2/_3$fl oz	1 tablespoon
30mL	1fl oz	1 tablespoon plus 2 teaspoons
60mL	2fl oz	$^1/_4$ cup
85mL	$2^1/_2$fl oz	$^1/_3$ cup
100mL	3fl oz	$^3/_8$ cup
125mL	4fl oz	$^1/_2$ cup
150mL	5fl oz	$^1/_4$ pint, 1 gill
250mL	8fl oz	1 cup
300mL	10fl oz	$^1/_2$ pint)
360mL	12fl oz	$1^1/_2$ cups
420mL	14fl oz	$1^3/_4$ cups
500mL	16fl oz	2 cups
600mL	20fl oz 1 pint,	$2^1/_2$ cups
1 litre	35fl oz $1^3/_4$ pints,	4 cups

Cup measurements

One cup is equal to the following weights.

	Metric	Imperial
Almonds, flaked	90g	3oz
Almonds, slivered, ground	125g	4oz
Almonds, kernel	155g	5oz
Apples, dried, chopped	125g	4oz
Apricots, dried, chopped	190g	6oz
Breadcrumbs, packet	125g	4oz

	Metric	Imperial
Breadcrumbs, soft	60g	2oz
Cheese, grated	125g	4oz
Choc bits	155g	5oz
Coconut, desiccated	90g	3oz
Cornflakes	30g	1oz
Currants	155g	5oz
Flour	125g	4oz
Fruit, dried (mixed, sultanas etc)	185g	6oz
Ginger, crystallised, glace	250g	8oz
Honey, treacle, golden syrup	315g	10oz
Mixed peel	220g	7oz
Nuts, chopped	125g	4oz
Prunes, chopped	220g	7oz
Rice, cooked	155g	5oz
Rice, uncooked	220g	7oz
Rolled oats	90g	3oz
Sesame seeds	125g	4oz
Shortening (butter, margarine)	250g	8oz
Sugar, brown	155g	5oz
Sugar, granulated or caster	250g	8oz
Sugar, sifted icing	155g	5oz
Wheatgerm	60g	2oz

Length

Some of us still have trouble converting imperial length to metric. In this scale, measures have been rounded off to the easiest-to-use and most acceptable figures.

To obtain the exact metric equivalent in converting inches to centimetres, multiply inches by 2.54 whereby 1 inch equals 25.4 millimetres and 1 millimetre equals 0.03937 inches.

Metric	Imperial
mm=millimetres	in = inches
cm=centimetres	ft = feet
5mm, 0.5cm	$^1/_4$in
10mm, 1.0cm	$^1/_2$in
20mm, 2.0cm	$^3/_4$in
2.5cm	1in
5cm	2in
8cm	3in
10cm	4in
12cm	5in
15cm	6in
18cm	7in
20cm	8in
23cm	9in
25cm	10in
28cm	11in
30cm	1 ft, 12in